FROM LINZ TO LANGLAND

A Journey with Ludwig Wittgenstein

A Play in Two Acts

by

Alan Sandry

Published by
Llyfrau Cambria Books, Wales, United Kingdom.
Cambria Books is an imprint of
Cambria Publishing Ltd.
Discover our other books at: www.cambriabooks.co.uk

Dramatis Personae

Professor Rhyddid *Narrator (Female, late 30's)*

Ludwig Wittgenstein *Philosopher (Male, mid 50's)*

Perkins *Cab Driver (Male, mid 50's)*

Mrs Mann *Landlady (Female, early 60's)*

Carwyn *Philosophy Student (Male, early 20's)*

Rebecca *Philosophy Student (Female, early 20's)*

Rush Rhees *Philosopher (Male, late 20's, early 30's)*

Saunders Lewis *Dramatist (Male, early 50's)*

Reverend Wynford Morgan Minister (Male, early 60's)

Mrs Mary Clement *Cook (Female, early 40's)*

Mr Albert Clement *Caulker (Male, mid 40's)*

Ben Richards *Medical Student (Male, 23)*

SETTING

Various locations around Swansea, Wales. Swansea Railway Station, Langland, Swansea University, Uplands, Brynmill.

TIME

The mid 1940's

ACT I

Scene 1: Swansea High Street Railway Station, 1940's (arrival)

Scene 2: Mrs Mann's house in Langland Road

Scene 3: Carwyn and Rebecca on Campus

Scene 4: Rush Rhees's office at Swansea University

ACT II

Scene 1: Ludwig Wittgenstein and Saunders Lewis

Scene 2: Cwmdonkin Terrace

Scene 3: The Famous Photograph

Scene 4: Ludwig Wittgenstein at Langland Bay

Scene 5: Swansea High Street Railway Station, 1940's (departure)

Act 1 Scene 1: *Swansea High Street Railway Station 1940's.*

Music: *Mozart Piano Sonata in C Major, No 16, K545, Allegro*

The left-hand side of the stage is lit in green and white. The rest of the stage is dark. Professor Rhyddid, smartly dressed, confident, enters from the right and comes to the left-hand side and gazes around at the audience.

She speaks with authority and precision.

PROFESSOR RHYDDID

Noswaith dda! Good evening! I am Professor Rhyddid, Philosophy Department. It is my pleasure… and my duty… to welcome you, be you novices or knowledge-laden, to Swansea; the university and the city, or town as was.

She smiles.

It is also my pleasure…and duty…to instruct you in the ways and methods of philosophy from the Ancients to the Moderns, from Logicians to Idealists, from Ethics to Epistemology, from Metaphysics to Aesthetics.

She pauses and looks intensively at the audience.

But I also want to welcome you to, as I see it, the intricate, perplexing, and often disordered world of the practitioners of philosophy, the philosophers themselves. Therefore, let us celebrate the Masters, and a few Mistresses, the inventors, the radicals, the game-changers. And when I talk about game-changers, and games in particular, there is no one more influential than Ludwig Wittgenstein.

So, let our journey begin at High Street Railway Station, one dark evening in the mid 1940's. A wartime environment, and the arrival of a genius.

Professor Rhyddid exits. The rest of the stage becomes lit. A mostly clear stage, with a bench to the right. A backdrop says "Swansea" in the style of a railway sign of the 1940's. Ludwig Wittgenstein enters in light grey trousers and a worn jacket with elbow pads, holding a tatty suitcase. He looks around, sniffs the air, and nervously starts to talk in a low voice.

LUDWIG

Ah! Swansea. The sea…. relaxation…. Rhees…. work.

He places his case on the ground, then wryly smiles.

And it is not Cambridge!

He pauses and smiles.

Am I glad to be here!

He again looks around and fumbles in his pocket. A man approaches. He is dressed in a dark suit with a peaked hat.

PERKINS

Hello Sir!

Perkins looks at a piece of paper.

Mr Watt Gone Stem, is it?

Ludwig looks unimpressed and bluntly replies.

LUDWIG

Wittgenstein! And you are?

PERKINS

I am Perkins, Sir. I am your cab driver. Mr Rhees from the university asked me to pick you up and deliver you to Langland Road, down The Mumbles. I assume that is correct, Sir?

LUDWIG

Yes. Thank you... That was good of Rhees. I will be with you...

Ludwig gestures to the exit.

Outside...shortly.

Perkins bows slightly.

PERKINS

No problem, Sir. At your convenience, Sir. Take your time, Sir. Take your time.

Perkins departs and Ludwig ponders.

LUDWIG

Take your time!

Ludwig scratches his head.

Time! What does he mean? I will take whatever time is needed to get to where he is, outside the station.

Ludwig looks around.

Time! Questions of time! Do trains run on time? Or do they run on rails? Or is it both? ... But how can one thing run on two separate things at the same time?

He pauses, then shakes his head.

Both are correct, but both are different. One question, two responses.

He puts his hand to the side of his head.

I need to answer that question more precisely.

He again fumbles in his pockets.

An enjoyable journey….no one bothered me. No talking…That is as I prefer it, as that means that I do not have any obligation to respond.

He walks towards the bench. Sits on it and looks around. The lighting changes. It brightens. Spotlight on Ludwig. It reflects the sun.

A beach offers hope. One can understand movement by observing the sea. It ebbs and flows. It operates to another natural rhythm; a non-man-made routine. It does not answer to anyone.

He again fiddles in his pockets. He is looking for something.

Why is life so predictable, yet so unknown? So much in tune, yet so atonal. Open to interpretation, but so often fixed and rigid.

He looks up. He points upwards and gesticulates towards the sky.

The sun…and the moon are with us each day. But what do we know of them? Do most people think about them when they rise…when they go to bed?

He shakes his head.

No! They do not feel any need to consider these, but they are the life givers. No need to think about what provides life. How can we… they….be so naïve. So ill informed.

He stands up, and again looks in his jacket.

I must ask Rhees.

He pulls out a pen.

Nothing is straightforward.

He pulls a tatty notebook from his left pocket, opens it, and reads it.

Notes! Notes for what? Notes towards a conclusion. Can we ever comprehensively conclude? Is there a final answer?

He shakes his head again, and walks about, thinking. He again reads the notebook.

Who will see these? I am alone in writing, but not in thought…. but maybe I am. Alone in thought, that is. But others play my game…. Russell. Carnap. Rhees.

He flicks through and peruses the notebook.

Words are my existence…sentences my blood flow…propositions are the only things that drive me, stir me, feed me.

He suddenly looks sad.

Is that all there is? Can I create more?

He wanders.

My mind...our minds require the uncovering of facts. Facts give us clarity. They ensure that we do not need further investigation. The facts about the sun, the moon, their axes, help us live our lives...unpolluted...simple.

He becomes exasperated.

But it is not simple, is it? It is intricate, delightful, evasive.

He beams with delight.

This must be discussed with Rhees.

He looks around and observes the sign that reads "Swansea".

Swansea is a release, a shaft of light. In this space I can work...not in that monotonous academic way...that Cambridge term-time method. Here I am allowed to express myself.

He half-smiles.

Hardly anybody knows me. Not even the academics recognise me. That is perfect. Lack of interference…. No nuisances or timewasters to avoid.

He wanders, still putting his hands in his pockets to search for something.

I must work! Those manuscripts….

He touches his mouth and wriggles his hand.

I will talk with Rhees. We must progress….no time to stall.

He smiles.

Back to time!

He sits down.

What makes me angry...distraught...is not knowing...no, it is not the knowing it is the means. I must calculate everything to achieve truth through accuracy...Verification is the key.

He smiles.

I try, but there just is not enough time. Time! Time! Time!...Cambridge presses down. It suppresses...it drains me. It has some advantages, but I often feel cocooned.

He gets up, pauses, and wanders.

How do we know so little? Three thousand years of philosophy...intensive discourse...great writers...poets...artists...scientists...mathematicians, but so little real progress. Very few definite answers. Progress may turn out to be a shutter to our world, and not the transparent gift that some imagine it to be.

He stops and looks up.

I must try harder.

He wanders around, searching in his pockets.

Should I have produced more? Here I am, a man in his 50's with so little to leave. A legacy...maybe? Of what? Who would read it? Who would understand it? They did not embrace the *Tractatus*.

He looks disappointed and wanders more. After some moments he looks a little more enthusiastic.

Swansea offers alternatives...lifestyles.... beauty...tranquillity. People are always telling me that the cultural scene is lively. The Kardomah Café attracted a salon set...and this Dylan Thomas character...making a name for himself as a wordsmith. I nearly caught him once at Cambridge. Missed him by a few days. I have read four or five of his poems, nine or ten minutes long. I prefer Rabindranath Tagore, but Thomas has something. He seems to understand nature...childhood.

He pauses and looks sad.

Ah, childhood!

He wiggles his finger in mid-air.

Let us not go there.

He pulls something out of his pocket. It is a piece of string. He looks at it, bemused. Then he returns it to his pocket.

Rhees is developing his thought. He is forging a reputation.

He looks around and gives an acknowledging smile.

This is a healthy domain. He will foster some young people; take matters forward.

He picks up his suitcase.

I should go...I think...I think, therefore I am.

He smiles acerbically.

Descartes. Dearly departed Descartes. I mention him though I have never really read him in detail…I know that I am here…here at Swansea Railway Station…

He ponders.

Wartime. Why do people do it? Fight, that is. A waste of their physical and mental capacities. We fight because we do not understand. The answers are not complete. They must be…they must be completed. Truth! Facts! Understanding!

Ludwig walks off.

Now, what is that man's name? Prosser? Porter?

He stops and looks aghast.

Popper?

He sighs as he remembers.

Perkins! That's it. Perkins!

He strolls off as lights dim.

Music: Brahms Opus 49, No 4 Lullaby

Act 1 Scene 2: *Mrs Mann's house in Langland Road.*

Professor Rhyddid enters and addresses the audience from the left side of the stage, which is lit with green and white lights. The rest of the stage is dark.

PROFESSOR RHYDDID

So, the great Ludwig Wittgenstein is in town…here, in Swansea…this evening. He is here for you and for me. Here to enlighten us, to challenge us, to make us look at things differently…or at least to reassess them and attempt to clarify them. He is in Perkins's cab, driving down the Mumbles Road, looking across the Bay, catching a glimpse of the Mumbles Train…Yes, we used to have one…Then he goes up Newton Road, snatching a view of Oystermouth Castle, before arriving at Langland Road…at his lodgings…at the congenial suburban home of Mrs Mann.

Professor Rhyddid exits, and the stage slowly lights up. Ludwig Wittgenstein is in his room at Mrs Mann's house in Langland Road. There is a plain bed. One chair is near the bed, alongside a bedside table with some books on it. There is a small clock on the table. Another chair is on the far side with a jacket on it. Ludwig sits on the bed, dressed in his shirt and trousers. He has a book in his hand. He is reading, then he looks around.

LUDWIG

Great literature…stimulates the mind. Poor literature…blows the mind, like dynamite. Merit is important, as is lucidity.

He ponders for a moment.

I do not read as much as others because I do not need to do so. My reading is selective.

He stands up and puts the book on the bed. He starts to stroll around.

Why are we inspired by some sayings, certain writing, particular places…. but other locations, people, collections of words leave us cold…stiff?

He ponders.

Is there an objective sense of quality? How do we evaluate the relationship between a person, their surroundings, and their tastes?

He scratches his head.

I prefer literature that informs me about tangible events …not merely theory or imagination. Most philosophers favour the latter…but I am an engineer, a mathematician…a theoretician yes, but that is only part of my canvas.

He walks around.

Should we classify? Does it affect our understanding if we put issues into boxes or segments, or if we place professions in order of rank? Hierarchy has burdens. Not everyone can meet the responsibilities, and rules of engagement, set for them.

He pauses and grimaces.

My family!

He sits on the chair, handles the books, and looks intensely at one of them.

If I read more, will that lead to my enlightenment? Will it enrich me? Or is conversation the route; the channel to enhanced behaviour and understanding?

He puts the book down and stands up.

Ultimately, I am doomed...my finite existence, as with every human body, means that I can only do so much. Can the bricklayer build a thousand houses by laying two million bricks, or is he bound by his physical abilities and technique? Willingness and age prevent him from achieving his goal. That is tragic.

Looking serious, he asks.

Should any of us have a goal?

He picks up one of the books and addresses it.

What interests me...no, infuriates me... is that these thoughts are not my thoughts. This...is not my art.

He looks at the clock on his table. He picks it up and shakes it. He looks at it curiously.

Time tells me that I must visit the university. Time for me to engage with Rhees. He may bring some colleagues, but I prefer it if I just speak with him. I only want to hear his opinions... Other people will simply distract us...they will not realise where I am...where we are...in our transaction.

He puts the clock back on the table and looks for his jacket. He finds it, puts it on, then sits back on the bed.

Do we really desire order? Order through time, perhaps? Time directs us.

He points in different directions.

Here at 9, across there at 10, in Rhees's office at 11…does that assist me?

He shakes his head. There is a knock.

Enter, please!

Mrs Mann enters from stage left. She has a pinafore over her clothes.

MRS MANN

Bore da Doctor Wittgenstein! Good morning! I hope you are well, and in good spirits. Would you like a nice cup of tea?

LUDWIG

No, not required…thank you!

MRS MANN

Are you sure? It will help you start the day. You are going out, I am guessing.

LUDWIG

That is not really a guess Mrs Mann. That is a definite intention, as I told you last evening.

MRS MANN

Well, whether you intend to be in or out, a hot cup of tea will get you started…put you in the right mood.

LUDWIG

Precisely how will a boiled beverage affect my mood...my contemplation?

MRS MANN

Well, it gets me going. A tasty brew. Two sugars. Welsh cake on the side.

LUDWIG

No thank you...

Ludwig holds his head then says in a polite but firm tone.

I beseech you to leave me alone...I must prepare.

MRS MANN

Oh, alright then...

She looks at him somewhat bemused.

I know that you like some peace and quiet.

LUDWIG

I must think...silence helps!

Mrs Mann starts to walk off.

I will not require an evening meal.

MRS MANN

Out all day then, is it?

LUDWIG

I will dine at the university.

MRS MANN

That is perfectly fine. But I will have some food here later if you change your mind.

Ludwig becomes irate.

LUDWIG

No, no, that is wrong. Why would I change my mind if I have spoken about dining elsewhere? Why would I be with you in this building when I will be three miles away at another location? There is no sense in that.

Mrs Mann puts out her arms in a calming gesture.

MRS MANN

It is not a problem Doctor Wittgenstein. I was only letting you know that I have food in. You do pay for it, remember.

LUDWIG

Yes, you are right. That is a fact. But I am not bound to this dining arrangement. I am not bound to anything.

Mrs Mann half-smiles and says in a calming voice.

MRS MANN

You come and go as you please cariad. I know that is how you like it. I will not disturb you anymore.

LUDWIG

Thank you!

Mrs Mann walks out, shaking her head. Ludwig stands up, then shuffles around.

I must go. I need to take a long walk...to think...before I see Rhees.

He plays around with his jacket, then brushes his hair with his hand.

Work must be undertaken. Rhees must listen to me. I have ideas and questions.... he must accommodate me.

He walks to the side.

I cannot waste this vacation. Time is precious. Only Rhees understands.... or attempts to understand.... I find that Swansea minds are more open than those of the pretentious dons who punt on the Cam.... Far fewer egos!

He turns around, walks to the table, picks up two books, and flicks through one. He then starts to walk off stage and says in a determined way.

To Rhees and to work.

Lights dim. Music: Schubert Serenade

Act 1 Scene 3: *Carwyn and Rebecca on Campus*

Professor Rhyddid enters stage right and addresses the audience from that side, which is lit in green and white. The rest of the stage is dark.

PROFESSOR RHYDDID

As our protagonist makes his way from Langland to Swansea University's Singleton campus, college life carries on as normal. Lectures, seminars, reading in the library, conversations on the footpaths, liaisons in the park...yes it all went on then, as it does now. Two exceptional students, Carwyn and Rebecca, are part of this tableau. Full of zest and inquiry, these students of philosophy have a plethora of questions to ask, many of which remain relevant today.

Professor Rhyddid exits. There is an empty stage, dimly lit. Two students enter from the left. Carwyn is dressed in a grey shirt with dark trousers. Rebecca is dressed in a white blouse with a pleated skirt. They are clutching books and briefcases.

CARWYN

That is another lecture over and done with.

REBECCA

Yes, only two more before the weekend.

CARWYN

How much of that did you understand?

REBECCA

Most of it, I think. Logical fallacies always confuse me. I know I should read more on that, but I am so busy with all the other things that we have been asked to digest.

Carwyn smiles and nods, acknowledging Rebecca's statement.

CARWYN

So, what do you make of this Wittgenstein fellow? Every time I see him, he appears to be shadowing Rush Rhees across campus.

REBECCA

He definitely seems to be an odd one...a bit like his writing.

CARWYN

Yes. I am surprised, though, that he does not want to talk with us.

REBECCA

That is his nature, so people say. A quiet one, something of a recluse!

CARWYN

But he likes fame and adulation, I am sure...like the rest of them.

Rebecca smiles

REBECCA

Is that what we should aim for?

CARWYN

What?

REBECCA

Fame and adulation. An entry in *Encyclopaedia Britannica* perhaps.

Rebecca laughs.

But I would hope for fortune as well. Recognition alone will not pay the bills.

CARWYN

Is that what you want? Isn't academic knowledge and the accolade of your peers enough?

REBECCA

Yes, but can't I have them all, and more? Why limit oneself? Why accept one prize?

Carwyn nods and smiles.

CARWYN

But is it a prize or a poisoned chalice?

Rebecca laughs.

REBECCA

Poisoned chalice! You and your bardolatry! I told you before that you should have concentrated on English Literature.

They both ponder. Rebecca sighs.

Why did you choose Philosophy over all the other subjects?

CARWYN

To get the answers, I suppose. The answers to all those questions that rattle around my grey matter.

REBECCA

So, have you got them? The answers to these mysterious questions.

CARWYN

Some...but not all.

REBECCA

Can you have them all?

CARWYN

Yes. That is if you read Wittgenstein.

They both laugh.

REBECCA

I have yet to do so.

Carwyn looks amazed.

CARWYN

What?

REBECCA

Read Wittgenstein.

Carwyn laughs.

I started, but...

CARWYN

I know!

REBECCA

It did not feed me enough. I did not gain my nutrients from within its pages.

CARWYN

Listen to you. You would think Wittgenstein was a chef.

REBECCA

For the mind, he probably is. It is just that my taste buds did not take to his specific flavours …. his quirky ingredients.

Carwyn laughs again, loudly.

CARWYN

Meaning you must get them elsewhere. Marx, perhaps? Or Locke? Or Plato?

REBECCA

I am more attuned to Héloïse or Wollstonecraft.

Carwyn looks at Rebecca in a smug way and says condescendingly.

CARWYN

Of course…the ladies.

REBECCA

The underrepresented women.

Carwyn smiles in a somewhat cynical manner and opens his hands in a gesture towards Rebecca.

CARWYN

Indeed! But in the great scheme of things, we must ask a vital question. Are they worthy?

REBECCA

Of what? Our recognition? Our attention? Our acceptance? If you wish to discard women, then we must return to the Suffragist debate.

Carwyn shakes his head.

CARWYN

I will accept that – the Equality for Women argument – but I am not sure about the contribution of female writers to the philosophical canon. Do they justify our attention? Are they important?

REBECCA

We are all important. Women no less so then the men you are forever praising and quoting.

CARWYN

But the difference is that they understand life. They can relate to our condition.

Rebecca looks dumbfounded.

REBECCA

And women do not?

Carwyn puts his hands together in a defensive gesture.

CARWYN

Women can contribute. I do not deny that, but not on men's issues...on the vital matters.

REBECCA

Namely?

Carwyn counts out on his fingers.

CARWYN

Government! Diplomacy! War! Leadership! Matters of State!

REBECCA

All the things that men mess up. The areas that men have dominated since time immemorial but which they still can't run with order.... with efficiency.

CARWYN

I do not claim perfection for these thoughts and acts.

REBECCA

Perfection! Chaos, bloodshed, and perpetual tragedy more like.

CARWYN

There are disciplines that suit women more than men.

Carwyn appeals to Rebecca.

Look at Wittgenstein with his talk of language and pictures. That is comprehensible by all.

REBECCA

By women with smaller brains, you mean.

CARWYN

No, you know that I don't mean that...I just think that we should not overstate the influence of girls on philosophy.

Rebecca is taken aback.

REBECCA

Girls now, are we?

CARWYN

Oh, you are hard to converse with when you are in this radical mood.

REBECCA

I think...and act...radically because conformity gets us nowhere. It is through challenging, verbally, and occasionally physically, that we are able to open the door towards progress.

CARWYN

It is all about that then, is it? Progress? Change?

REBECCA

Yes, change for the better. Social amelioration. A better world, away with the ashes of this horrible war...a place that facilitates the fostering of respect and toleration.

CARWYN

Toleration...oh, we are back to Locke.

REBECCA

We can read him, of course, but this is our world Carwyn. Take Locke on board as much as we do the others, including Wittgenstein, but remember that it is you, me and our fellow students who are the future. We can shape this world, saving the best from the past, whilst proclaiming our demands. Hope! Peace! Equality!

Carwyn shakes his head and turns slightly.

CARWYN

You dreamer.

REBECCA

Perhaps I am. I do not reject that, but it is better to dream than to be defeated by those who you know are wrong...who you know have failed.

Carwyn smiles They both look up and around. Carwyn produces a copy of Wittgenstein's Tractatus and turns to Rebecca.

CARWYN

For now, we need to read this. Let us see what points we can raise with Mr. Rhees. Who knows, we may even get to meet the great Ludwig Wittgenstein.

They both smile and laugh as they walk off.

Lights dim.

Music: *Mahler Piano Quarter in A minor*

Act 1 Scene 4: Rush Rhees's office at Swansea University

Professor Rhyddid enters from the right and approaches the centre of the stage which is lit in green and white. The rest of the stage is dark.

PROFESSOR RHYDDID

Swansea University...Here! Us! Wittgenstein's occasional home...or perhaps, deep down, his favourite other home from whichever other place he called home...at that moment in time...if that makes sense. His friend, and former student, Rush Rhees is here. A commanding philosopher in his own right, Rhees is Wittgenstein's sidekick. The Watson to his Holmes, maybe, or perhaps the Sancho Panza to his Don Quixote? Either way, he is a man with a formidable mind, who acted as interlocutor and amanuensis to Wittgenstein; both praising his ideas, and dampening his expectations, in equal measure. His office was across the way.

She points out.

And it is there that we find the two philosophers.

Professor Rhyddid exits. The stage lights up. There is a desk and chair in the back with a typewriter on the desk. Rush Rhees sits at a chair, looking relaxed, with pen in hand. He is writing in a notebook. Ludwig Wittgenstein sits opposite, vigilant but on edge.

RHEES

Did you sleep well Wittgenstein? Are you refreshed?

LUDWIG

Partly!

He hesitates and thinks.

That is my answer to both of your questions.

RHEES

Not fully then?

LUDWIG

Am I ever fully refreshed? I dry up…you know that. Who does not?

RHEES

Indeed! Though can we ever be 100% of anything? Can we ever reach the maximum in terms of attentiveness and momentum?

LUDWIG

But if we do not try, if we allow ourselves too much latitude then we will never succeed.

Pause. Ludwig strokes his hair whilst Rhees keeps on working.

RHEES

Tell me honestly, do these conversations help or hinder?

LUDWIG

Help, of course!

RHEES

I am pleased. They aid me, as well. They always have done.

LUDWIG

You must move along Rhees, you must diverge. The welding was good for you. Very good! It enabled a different thought-process to come to the fore. You are a man who is studious, yet your nature and intelligence allow for flexibility. I have tried this approach, but only certain things bring me succour.

RHEES

Such as? As if I did not know.

LUDWIG

Those close to me...Solitude...Norway is always a comfort...and stimulating. The bays of the Gower...

Ludwig smiles.

Incredibly alluring.

RHEES

A combination that nurtures your work...your writing and teaching.

LUDWIG

But is it enough? Should I have published more? The *Tractatus* now represents just one stage, only an epoch. I thought that it would have been the final word, but things alter...unfortunately!

RHEES

So, you must make more material available.

LUDWIG

With your help!

RHEES

You have it, of course, but the timing...the moment for release must be yours.

Ludwig contemplates.

LUDWIG

I understand. But it must be perfect. This time there cannot be any penumbras.

RHEES

There will forever be grey areas. We accept that, don't we?

LUDWIG

No! There must not be. Their existence must be scratched...eradicated. We need a transparent code...for language, for reading...for philosophy...though that is the least of my concerns.

RHEES

Hence, philosophy follows language in precedence.

LUDWIG

Yes, it must. Philosophical questions, problems, and debates all crumble if our language is pure and comprehensible. I explained that in the *Tractatus*.

RHEES

So that is that. No need for any further explanation.

LUDWIG

Rhees, please. Not you! ...All is not said. There are holes...gaps in our language and knowledge.

RHEES

Therefore, you must fill them. Use your pencil to fill in the blanks... to join the dots! Look for more evidence. I told you before, you should read more Hume.

Ludwig stands up. He is clearly frustrated and holds his head.

You know that I am available...at all times.

LUDWIG

Yes, and I am grateful...You are a fine sounding board. You have absorbed so much.

RHEES

From you!

Ludwig looks round and becomes excitable.

LUDWIG

What is missing? What further tools do we require...to slot it all together...to stoke the cognitive fire.

RHEES

Do you mean words? Grammar? Thought? What components?

LUDWIG

All those...and so much more, I feel.

Rhees gestures in a 'me and you' fashion.

RHEES

Does this open the mental passage?

LUDWIG

What? My time with you. My moments in Swansea.

RHEES

Yes, all of that. Think of it as the package that assists enquiry.

LUDWIG

But is it the right package?

They both contemplate for a few moments. Rhees makes some notes as Ludwig walks around.

Yesterday I walked along the seafront. I was not sure if the tide was ebbing or flowing. Why didn't I know? That is basic.

RHEES

But not straightforward. You would have needed to observe the sea for quite a while...or to have asked a fisherman?

LUDWIG

But I should have known. That is a fact. The movement of the tides are set...our knowledge of gravitational forces allows us to produce tables. We can use our clocks and watches to visualise the movements. The sea is not static, like the clouds, or time itself. I should have known.

RHEES

One cannot know everything.

LUDWIG

Why not?

Ludwig points at Rhees.

Solve that one...or ask your students to do so.

A moment of contemplation. Rhees makes more notes. Ludwig strokes his chin.

These issues...problems...dilemmas must be solved. Then I must write down the answers to display them to the world. Everybody...everybody should know whether that tide was making its way towards us, or whether it was departing us. Everybody!

RHEES

Education and inspiration could be the solution. Socrates was trying to get people to reach an understanding that was their own.

Rhees leans forward.

Know thyself!

Ludwig sighs, scratches his head, and looks frustrated.

Do you want a drink? Some tea?

LUDWIG

You say the same as my landlady.

RHEES

A simple question!

LUDWIG

But is that your role in life now? An academic, an intellectual, asking me if I want to drink some tea. Rhees, my fine friend, you are becoming so...Welsh.

RHEES

Right, no tea...let us just continue.

LUDWIG

Do we have anything to say? And if we do, can we say it before that tide turns?

RHEES

Is that what bothers you? The tide! ...Is that the fulcrum? Does it all depend on the moon controlling the tides?

LUDWIG

Perhaps!

Rhees stands up, looking frustrated. Ludwig then sits down.

I need to know...Too many holes in my thought, too many unresolved matters.

Rhees sits back down, then offers his notebook to Ludwig.

RHEES

Write them down!

LUDWIG

Write what down?

RHEES

These unresolved matters, these holes in your thought...write them down and work them through...numerically and logically!

LUDWIG

Will it mean that they will be gone forever? Will it mean that those questions burst like a superfluous balloon, never to return to ascend the sky or to blur our vision?

RHEES

They may!

LUDWIG

But Rhees, tell me, is that enough to make me write... in your notebook...with your pencil? Is it really?

RHEES

If it solves the problem, then yes...that is what you must do.

LUDWIG

Did Schopenhauer?

RHEES

Why bring him into our dialogue?

Ludwig points out towards the coast, and loudly states.

LUDWIG

He will have seen those tides. He will have contemplated their schedule. Schopenhauer will have worked out the ebb and the flow.

RHEES

But it would have been a different tidal pattern...unless he visited Swansea.

LUDWIG

No! The place would have been different, but the scientific variations remain the same.

RHEES

The water would not be the same. Its chemical make-up would not be that of the water you saw last night.

LUDWIG

You are wrong. The chemical components are the same, but the actual drops of water, and how they are affected by elements around them, are not...at least we think they are not.

Rhees scratches his head.

RHEES

Does this have any bearing?

LUDWIG

Of course! We are both human beings, with similar genetics, but we are completely unalike.

RHEES

Completely...?

LUDWIG

In most aspects, yes! We must divide sameness from similarities.

RHEES

But will that answer your question...your dilemma as to which cycle of the sea you observed?

LUDWIG

It must do...there are only two options...either in or out.

RHEES

So, now all questions – all problems – must be stripped down to fundamental binary positions. Do we use Occam's razor?

LUDWIG

We have confused ourselves, and others, for millennia. Let us not look for things that are not there. The tide is a perfect example. In? Or out? No hidden agenda. No third choice. No magical element. Purity! That is what we must tell and show the world. That is our duty.

RHEES

Now we are getting somewhere...I shall propose tea more often!

Ludwig looks bemused.

These conundrums, and your solutions, must be enunciated... This is your next major work Ludwig!

LUDWIG

Or will it be? Am I washed up?

He looks to one side and sarcastically mumbles.

Like those tides!

He looks intensively at Rhees.

Sometimes, at Cambridge, I feel cornered. Here, in this environment, I am liberated. I sense that I am attempting to break free of the bondage.

RHEES

Of which Rousseau warned us.

He leans towards Ludwig and says reassuringly.

Stay here then...for as long as you like.

LUDWIG

I am limited…tied in…my time at Swansea is precious, and it is appealing to imagine that I could spend more days with you in this milieu…But there are matters that I must resolve at Cambridge.

RHEES

Wittgenstein, please write. The world of philosophy needs you to present more in literary form. Students in the years ahead can read you, interpret you, refine you.

Ludwig looks up to the sky. He is unconvinced.

LUDWIG

Ah! But how can you refine facts. They exist. They are.

RHEES

Does that mean that your work – our work – is set in stone?

LUDWIG

He raises his voice and adamantly states.

Facts are facts Rhees. There is not any refinement required.

They both sit and contemplate for a few moments.

RHEES

Will you dine here today?

LUDWIG

First drink then food. You and Mrs Mann are alike in so many ways.

Pause

RHEES

I simply wish to ascertain whether you will join me in the Common Room, or if you have other plans?

LUDWIG

Almost certainly.

RHEES

What?

LUDWIG

Both!

RHEES

They will be serving lamb this evening.

LUDWIG

Lamb in Wales! A certainty...like the tides!

Pause

RHEES

Do you wish to work more, or are you tired? Did you really get some sleep last night?

LUDWIG

A minimal amount.

RHEES

Minimal! Which is?

LUDWIG

Several hours...it is not a debatable point.

RHEES

Well, if you tire you can always sleep on that chair with this one for your feet. Or go back to your lodgings for a period.

LUDWIG

Neither will be necessary. We must crack on with work...then further down the line... after tides, Schopenhauer, Rousseau, words, sentences, commas, asterisks, and mathematical equations we will move...logically...on to lamb.

Lights dim.

Music: Schoenberg 6 Piano Pieces Opus 19

Act 2 Scene 1: *Ludwig Wittgenstein and Saunders Lewis*

Music: *Schoenberg 6 Piano Pieces Opus 19 (short reprise)*

Professor Rhyddid enters from the right and addresses the audience from the left, which is spotlighted in green and white.

PROFESSOR RHYDDID

Universities are cauldrons of discussion, covens of debate, and manifestations of intrigue.

She points at the audience, gestures, and cackles.

I will not go as far as saying that they are a nest of vipers, but you get my drift. These are the places where interesting people meet, and ideas collide. The Big Bang! The fireworks of thought! When the likes of Ludwig Wittgenstein wander the campus, they inevitably encounter other fascinating minds. Some ignore them, some seek to engage. Few know who the curious looking man is, others are oblivious to his greatness. So, what are we to expect when, one moonlit evening, Ludwig chances upon the dramatist, literary critic and prominent political activist, Saunders Lewis?

Professor Rhyddid exits. Bare stage. Evening on Campus. Dimly lit, but with a spot where the moon is shining down. Saunders Lewis, dressed in a suit with a dickie bow, is meandering, whilst Wittgenstein comes towards him in a hurry. Saunders, looking anxious, stops Ludwig in his tracks.

SAUNDERS

Noswaith dda! Beth yw'r amser?

Wittgenstein looks surprised.

LUDWIG

I am sorry! Why is your "arm sore"?

SAUNDERS

Ah!

Saunders giggles nervously

What time is it, Sir?

LUDWIG

Time…?

Ludwig looks around, shaking his head.

Time is only relevant in certain circumstances.

Saunders smiles

SAUNDERS

I must remember that. Ardderchog! Da iawn!

LUDWIG

You must ask somebody else. I avoid timepieces.

SAUNDERS

A bold idea. I like that.

Saunders raises his finger, wags it and smiles.

A pre-modern decision.

LUDWIG

Every idea must be practical. The deliberate decision to avoid holding and maintaining a watch allows me to think without the obvious constraint of time...at least when I am in this town.

SAUNDERS

You are not from Swansea then!

Saunders points at Ludwig and smiles.

I traced the accent...Germany or Austria?

LUDWIG

Austrian...by birth.

SAUNDERS

The land of Mozart and Gustav Klimt.

Ludwig abruptly intervenes.

LUDWIG

I knew him…Klimt that is, not Mozart…naturally that would be impossible!

Saunders ponders and stares.

SAUNDERS

You are not that philosopher by any chance, are you? Wittgenstein?

LUDWIG

Yes, that is me.

Saunders holds out his hand.

SAUNDERS

A great pleasure to meet you.

They shake hands. Saunders enthusiastically, Ludwig less so.

I am Saunders Lewis, formerly of the Welsh Department. I am here to visit an old colleague, a trusted friend.

LUDWIG

I do not work here…perhaps that is a pity.

SAUNDERS

You are visiting Rush Rhees. I had heard about your relationship.

LUDWIG

He is a fine man and a philosopher with whom I share many considerations.

SAUNDERS

We all need those...brethren who have the same body and soul instincts.

LUDWIG

And mind, of course. Descartes would never forgive us for forgetting that element of ourselves.

Saunders laughs and smiles. He points and indicates off stage.

SAUNDERS

Would you care to join me for an aperitif Professor Wittgenstein?

LUDWIG

That is a kind question...a human gesture!

SAUNDERS

So, is that a yes?

LUDWIG

I cannot, I am afraid. I must arrange things...this evening.

SAUNDERS

You are busy. I completely understand.

LUDWIG

I am trying to create and formulate as much as I can in this limited, precious space. I am attempting to shape certain propositions...to ensure perspicuity!

SAUNDERS

The best of luck. I am sure you will succeed.

Ludwig leans towards Saunders and asks inquisitively.

LUDWIG

Do you have plans and intellectual maps that demand clarification?

Saunders smiles.

SAUNDERS

I do, but mine are very different to yours. Mine are dramatic in their construction. Logic is secondary. I have characters to portray my thoughts. They are my conduit to that world. I would proffer that they are my cerebral and everyday channels to the world.

LUDWIG

I must read your output. We can all learn something from each other, although I am drawn to the conclusion that we complicate our lives with peripheral elements.

Saunders laughs.

SAUNDERS

Some say Wales is peripheral...as a place, and *Cymry* as a people.

Ludwig shakes his head and states firmly.

LUDWIG

No, that is not the case.

SAUNDERS

I will hold you to that defence, Professor. Life is a struggle, albeit a pleasant one when you are imagining a world that does not have the rigid chains of industrialisation wrapped around it.

LUDWIG

My father was an industrialist, a steel magnate.

Saunders comes nearer and asks inquisitively.

SAUNDERS

With principles?

Ludwig ponders for a moment.

LUDWIG

Yes, we all have them, though our interpretation of someone else's may be open for debate.

Saunders mops his brow and looks thoughtfully at Ludwig.

What will this life be like then? This Arcadia, of which you speak.

SAUNDERS

It will be one where the idea of freedom is to the fore. Where the *Cymry* – the Welsh people – can express themselves through all the cultural forms, in their own language, with their own kith and kin.

LUDWIG

One language, one understanding and sentiment.

Ludwig thinks and appears unsure.

Is it really that simple?

SAUNDERS

Life is not simple, but unity, and a yearning for communal concord, is.

LUDWIG

If you wish to unite, presumably?

SAUNDERS

The Welsh people do...though they sometimes fall short in their expression of that desire.

LUDWIG

People always "fall short", as you observe. They are distracted by matters that they cannot resolve or should not even take on board. They look for complex metaphysical answers to the simplest of concerns. They blind themselves to what is in their eye line. Myopia pervades!

Ludwig bends a little and looks fatigued.

SAUNDERS

You are a fascinating man.

Ludwig shrugs

Rhees is honoured to have you as a friend and collaborator.

LUDWIG

He listens! He challenges!

SAUNDERS

But in a positive way...not in the negative, debilitating way in which certain forces attack me.

LUDWIG

I am disappointed to hear that. Why would anybody use such tactics?

SAUNDERS

I have the British State against me.

Saunders moves his head and proclaims.

Imperialists dislike dissenters.

Ludwig smiles and shrugs his shoulders.

In your discipline you merely have orthodox philosophers, who do not allow your views into their domains.

Ludwig forcibly interjects.

LUDWIG

Their Weltanschauung.

Saunders nods his head in agreement.

SAUNDERS

Whilst I have politicians of the Empire; people who relish in the memories and realities of the usurpation of Wales. Sadly, there are some here who pledge allegiance to those very leaders who suppress us.

LUDWIG

So, it is political history that acts as the centre point of your ideology?

SAUNDERS

History is today. Without a sense of real, tangible freedom, and without a well-lit pathway ahead, the ghosts of history will remain the opponents of my people.

LUDWIG

Beautifully contended…. dramatically, but gracefully, espoused!

Saunders turns slightly, clenches his fist, and says in a determined but controlled voice.

SAUNDERS

I will always fight for my civilisation, and argue for the place, and the justice, of my people.

LUDWIG

With eloquence….

Short silence, before Saunders suddenly remembers that he was seeking the time.

SAUNDERS

I have kept you. I asked you the time, and we never discovered what it is.

LUDWIG

It is later than when you asked.

Saunders laughs.

SAUNDERS

I am uninformed regarding the time, but I have been enlightened by our crisp dialogue. Will you be here long?

LUDWIG

Without a watch, I cannot say.

Saunders smiles

SAUNDERS

In Abertawe I mean.

Ludwig cracks a gentle smile.

LUDWIG

A short period more. I have been here several weeks already, but I have commitments elsewhere.

SAUNDERS

Perhaps we will meet again, Sir. I certainly hope so.

LUDWIG

With that I will concur.

Ludwig smiles and Saunders holds out his hand. They shake.

SAUNDERS

Hwyl fawr Professor Wittgenstein!

LUDWIG

Thank you and goodbye Mr Lewis!

They walk past each other and off the stage.

Music: Massenet - Thaïs, DO 24, Act II: "Méditation"

Act 2 Scene 2: Cwmdonkin Terrace

Professor Rhyddid enters and address the audience from the middle of the stage, which is lit in green and white.

PROFESSOR RHYDDID

Wittgenstein arrives in the Uplands, Swansea's bohemian neighbourhood, home to writers and wranglers. Also, home to the Reverend Wynford Morgan, man of the cloth, and his dutiful wife Mrs Morgan, plus their neighbours Mr Albert Clement and Mrs Mary Clement, caulker and canteen worker alike. Just across the road is the property that for 23 years housed the Thomas family. Their son, Dylan, has done well for himself. Publishing his poetry and working for the BBC, wouldn't you know? That is something special. Ludwig would lodge at both the homes of Reverend and Mrs Morgan, and Mr and Mrs Clement, and would spend countless hours sitting, eating, conversing, and arguing, with the Reverend in particular. Ludwig was comfortable and at ease in Cwmdonkin Terrace, where he was extremely well fed at the hands of Mary Clement, and where the Clement daughters, Barbara and Joan, gave him an affectionate sobriquet.

Professor Rhyddid exits. There is a table and four chairs on the stage. Albert and Mary Clement are present, with Reverend Morgan and Ludwig Wittgenstein. The men are sitting at the table which has some crockery and cutlery on it and Mrs Clement is shuffling some dishes of food. Albert is glancing through a newspaper.

Mary looks at Ludwig.

MARY

You are looking glum today.

Ludwig looks at Mary with a mix of surprise and annoyance.

LUDWIG

Glum? Well, I am concerned...perhaps my face is writing that word in your mind.

Mary Looks amazed and smiles.

It is an era of war, and great loss.

MARY

Yes! Very sad times. But we must keep going.

Pause. Ludwig looks intensely at Mary.

LUDWIG

Your food is nourishing and plentiful.

MARY

Thank you, Vicky. Eat up now!

Ludwig looks humble.

LUDWIG

Yes, yes. I will eat my required amount, and it will invigorate me.

MARY

That's right, and you will then be able to scribble things in that old notebook of yours.

Ludwig looks knowingly, raises his shoulders and half-smiles.

LUDWIG

I write when I need to, but speech is my primary tool. If people listen, then ponder, that is easier for them, and for me, rather than seeing them reading and then dismissing, or misunderstanding, the meaning, or the message in the words.

Mary stretches in silence. Then she gently taps Ludwig.

MARY

You are right. I tell the girls in the canteen something and they listen. The same with Mr Clement!

Mary turns her head and stares at Albert.

He listens to me...most of the time. But if I write something down, he will ignore it or rip it up.

LUDWIG

But is the message communicated? That is the fundamental question.

The Reverend looks up from his plate.

REVEREND

It is the same with me, from the pulpit.

LUDWIG

And your pulpit allows you the powerbase for your sermonising Reverend.

The Reverend laughs.

REVEREND

My pulpit is your lectern Ludwig.

Ludwig wags his finger dismissively then says.

LUDWIG

But you preach, and I teach.

Ludwig becomes intense and bolts forward.

A world of difference. Your vertical instruction contrasting my horizontal interaction.

REVEREND

We both pass on our knowledge in good faith.

LUDWIG

But I deal in facts not assertions about other lives...beyond this one, which I am living and experiencing.

Mary hovers then moves forward.

MARY

Another cup of tea Vicky?

She turns and looks across.

Reverend?

Both men smile and gesture that they do not require anything else. Mary departs.

REVEREND

My God...our God... is all about truth, and compassion for all souls.

LUDWIG

Compassion...through death and sacrifice, and ridicule and humiliation.

REVEREND

Through giving his only son to shine the light and show us the path.

Ludwig pushes his chest out.

LUDWIG

The path to where?

REVEREND

Salvation and a better eternal existence.

Ludwig gestures with his hands out

LUDWIG

Here?

Ludwig points upwards.

Or there?

REVEREND

Everywhere Ludwig. Omnipotence and omniscience. It is the belief in improving our lives through immersing ourselves in the ways and teachings of our Lord.

LUDWIG

Belief! On what basis?

The Reverend looks unsure. Ludwig continues, sitting forward and holding up his fingers.

Is it scientific? Analytical? Are we considering a God...a Lord, as you say...who has worked out detail?

REVEREND

Everything is worked out.

Ludwig puts his hands on his head.

LUDWIG

It cannot be. Too many contradictions. So many misunderstandings.

REVEREND

Not if you believe Ludwig.

Ludwig shakes his head and brings down his hands.

Turn off your tap of curiosity Ludwig and have faith in our ultimate destiny.

LUDWIG

Which is what Reverend? Submission? Subjugation? Or merely a state of false consciousness?

REVEREND

A true mind Ludwig. A free existence in a world of unbounded beauty.

LUDWIG

Impossible without understanding! Inconceivable without knowledge and certainty...without science, mathematics, and the clarity of our language.

REVEREND

But the Bible provides those answers.

Ludwig moves forward slightly and laughs.

LUDWIG

The words of an ancient esoteric text. How can that possibly relate to the language of modern life? The discursive game that you and I are playing now...in Swansea, in Wales in the middle of the Twentieth Century.

REVEREND

It applies across time. It is an infinite set of judgements.

LUDWIG

But it does not provide the answers.

Albert slowly stands up.

ALBERT

We may never know the answer.

LUDWIG

We cannot stop asking the questions Albert. It is the same as your work. You are continuously repairing the ships. I am locked into my world of pondering the problems of language...talking with Rhees...making notes. Seeking to understand. Your work is unfeigned, it is invaluable. It is practical and fulfilling. Mine is temporary. It is absorbing but frustrating.

Ludwig looks across and points.

And the Reverend must believe in his distant Lord to satisfy his soul, and those of his parish. But it is not solid, it is symbolic. It is like the chocolate that melts in my cup of cocoa.

REVEREND

No, no, no Ludwig. It is my inner understanding, in my head and in my heart...and yes, it is in my soul, and the souls of others.

LUDWIG

That is insufficient Reverend. You cannot command people to walk along the tightrope with their eyes closed and then tell them to have faith that they do not fall to their death.

Ludwig stands up.

We must have certitude.

Ludwig points at Reverend Morgan.

You think you know, but your thought...your belief...is like the mist. It drifts around us, but it lacks substance and solidity.

REVEREND

I have peace of mind Ludwig. Something you appear to lack.

Ludwig shakes his head vigorously and smiles.

LUDWIG

Is that your answer...to life? To everything?

Ludwig turns to Albert and holds his hands out towards him.

And you Albert. Do you have peace of mind?

Albert thinks as he puts down his paper.

ALBERT

I sleep well if that is what you mean? Like a log!

Ludwig pointing to Albert.

LUDWIG

You have clarity and understanding of your role, that is why. I have not.

Ludwig looks at Reverend Morgan and gestures.

And he certainly cannot because his books contain a large dose of mythology.

Reverend Morgan smiles.

REVEREND

They are mystical, undoubtedly, but not mythological.

LUDWIG

How can you say that? Those stories eschew facts. Their purpose is to instil imagery into the muddled minds of their adherents.

REVEREND

The Ten Commandments are not imagery Ludwig. They are God's instructions for our lives....the actual words of God in stone.

LUDWIG

So where can I find these stones Reverend? Please tell me their location and I will travel to view them. I shall take Ben and he can capture these stones on film.

REVEREND

You know that they are hidden in the Ark of the Covenant Ludwig.

Ludwig puts his hand to his mouth.

It comes down to belief through knowledge, or vice versa.

Ludwig looks in despair, then firmly states.

LUDWIG

An impossibility without facts, data, statistics. You cannot convince me of this loose, ungrounded system.

REVEREND

Sadly, that is your loss Ludwig. Though there is still time for you to accept the Lord. He doesn't go anywhere.

The Reverend looks at Ludwig and asks in a precise manner.

Do you believe in God Ludwig?

Ludwig contemplates for a moment.

LUDWIG

Yes, I do, but the difference between what you believe and what I believe may be infinite.

Ludwig moves his body forward.

I admire Leo Tolstoy's magnificent work, *The Gospel in Brief,* in which he strips away the supernatural miracles and informs us about Jesus's role as a teacher, as in the Sermon on the Mount. Here he is conveying principles and values, which can assist us practically.

Ludwig looks at Reverend Morgan and gestures.

No sign of a burning bush...or Jonah surviving in the fish's belly.

Silence as Ludwig and Reverend Morgan look at each other. Albert rises and pulls up his braces.

ALBERT

God or no God, I must get ready for my shift. I know that is real, and if I am late the foreman will dock my pay.

Mary enters.

And Mary will not be amused at that.

Mary looks somewhat perplexed.

I am going in a moment love. Give Joan and Barbara a big cwtch from me.

Mary nods and smiles

MARY

Your sandwiches are in the kitchen Albert. Cheese and pickle!

Albert kisses Mary on the cheek.

ALBERT

You really are an angel.

Albert turns towards Ludwig and chuckles.

Oh, I am sorry Vicky!

Reverend Morgan smiles as Ludwig looks on intensely.

Music: Yves Guilbert The Keys of Heaven

Act 2: Scene 3: *The Famous Photograph.*

Professor Rhyddid enters from the left and addresses the audience from the right, which is lit in green and white.

PROFESSOR RHYDDID

Though Ludwig was content spending time with the inhabitants of Cwmdonkin Terrace, he was delighted when his partner, Ben Richards, decided to visit Swansea in 1947. Apart from wishing to spend time with Ludwig, Ben also wanted to see the sights of Swansea. Hence, they would venture to Mumbles, Gower and around the urban areas. They spent many hours on the seafront, and it was here, at Brynmill Station, that Ben took the famous 'Wittgenstein at Swansea' photograph.

Professor Rhyddid exits. Brynmill Station shelter is slowly revealed as the stage lights rise. A wooden building with a dividing concrete wall. The wall is heavily graffitied. Ludwig and Ben are standing with the wall in the background. Ben is holding a camera.

LUDWIG

I told you it was impressive.

BEN

You did, and as ever you were right.

LUDWIG

The Mumbles Train stops here, and it is so near the beach.

Ludwig gestures towards the beach at the back. He then turns and points in the opposite direction.

Up there is Bryn Road, where I first stayed with Rhees in 1942. From my room I could look out at the sea, and I would watch the Mumbles Train and the other mainline trains pass by.

BEN

Fond memories then.

LUDWIG

Memories are good Ben, but the present, with you, is sublime.

Ludwig looks at Ben and they both smile.

It is good that you have brought the camera.

Ben holds up the camera and looks at it.

Do photographs tell us anything about the serious questions?

BEN

Probably not Ludwig. They capture our clothes and moods at specific moments in time. They show whether we know how to smile or scowl, laugh, or cry. They witness our human condition.

Ben holds the camera to his eye. Ludwig frowns.

LUDWIG

Those mundane things. What a disappointment. But because I do not want to be identified or recognised by my facial expressions alone, I must ask, in consequential terms, how will the camera capture me my dear Ben?

Ludwig juggles his hands.

Am I a modernist?

Ludwig shrugs his shoulders.

Am I an archaeologist of language?

Ludwig gently laughs.

Am I an Austrian man who is a long way from the city of his birth? Am I a philosopher, or a mathematician, or an architect, or a teacher, or a gardener, or a hospital porter? Am I one of those or all of them.

Ludwig laughs a little louder.

How can I be all of them? Substance or semantics. What shall I choose? If we bring it down to emotions and outlooks, then am I a man of sadness or a man of joy?

Ludwig laughs louder.

Will I be remembered as a man of joy?

Ludwig scratches his head and laughs to himself.

Will I be remembered at all, and if so in what form? This architect from Austria, this logician from Linz, this scholar from Skjolden, this advocate of cognition from Cambridge, this Philosopher of Mind from Manchester.

Ludwig laughs aloud.

This splendid photographer's subject from Swansea.

BEN

And I will capture you in all your guises.

They both laugh.

LUDWIG

But will it be authentic? Will it reflect the inner Ludwig, or will we merely glance the outer Wittgenstein? The Wittgenstein of the stage, of the lecture theatre.

BEN

Will that depend upon who sees it and who interprets it in whatever way?

LUDWIG

Ah, my dear Ben. You suggest that it may come down to a question of credibility. Their eyes against mine, or against ours, as we are here at Brynmill Station, Swansea at this moment in time.

Ludwig holds his hands up high.

In AD 1947. Is that so?

BEN

Possibly. You understand these matters better than I Ludwig. What do you think? What do you want? Shall I take the photograph or not?

LUDWIG

You must Ben. Then I shall take one of you. I can also be a photographer. It is another of my guises, as you say.

They both laugh and they reach out to touch hands.

BEN

You should try to project an image of yourself that you want the world to see.

LUDWIG

Back to authenticity, are we? Project myself! I will try. You must capture the immanent Wittgenstein, Ben.

Ludwig poses and smiles in a silly manner.

How is this?

BEN

Definitely not! That is blasé.

Ludwig looks sad.

That is better but try to look somewhere in between those two poses.

Ludwig straightens his body and neck and adopts a facial pose that splits emotions.

That's it. Hold that. Don't move.

Ludwig holds his position as Ben snaps.

LUDWIG

What did that look like?

BEN

Like Mona Lisa on Swansea promenade.

They both laugh out loud. Ludwig gives Ben a gentle hug.

LUDWIG

When you produce the photographs Ben, we must cut them to eradicate the background.

BEN

No! I disagree Ludwig. The background is perfect. It gives perspective. There is writing and etchings on that wall that fit neatly with who you are Ludwig; what you are interested in. Your skill. They show language as art.

LUDWIG

You are kind Ben, but I will have to look at the finished photographed. I will judge it before I cut it. But I like the idea that the languages and symbols of other people are behind and around us. So, we may keep this photograph just as you took it…if it pleases us.

They gently laugh and Ben hands the camera to Ludwig. Ben adopts Ludwig's position and vice versa.

Will you mimic my position, Ben?

Ben moves his body to face left.

BEN

No!

They both laugh.

I cannot mimic you Ludwig. You are unique.

LUDWIG

We are all unique Ben. You most certainly are. You have a beautiful mind and body and are so sweet. To me, you are a satyr.

Ben giggles and poses his body.

BEN

Danke Herr Doktor Wittgenstein!

Ludwig laughs.

Lights dim.

Music: Debussy Clair de Lune

Act 2 Scene 4: *Ludwig Wittgenstein at Langland Bay*

Professor Rhyddid enters from the right and addresses the audience from the left, which is lit in green and white.

PROFEESOR RHYDDID

Whilst these frivolities on the promenade, and the discussions in houses and university rooms, are all well and good, everybody needs some time out, a period to chill. Everybody needs time to think, and to relax. Nobody more than Ludwig Wittgenstein. And there is no greater place for contemplation than Swansea and Gower. Close to his lodgings are some resplendent beaches. He could walk downhill from Cwmdonkin Terrace to Swansea Bay. Moreover, a ten-minute stroll from Mrs Mann's would take Ludwig to Langland Bay...

She ponders for a moment.

Ludwig... Langland... Language... mmm, a pattern emerges.

She smiles.

To Langland it is then, to join our philosopher magnifique!

Professor Rhyddid exits. A bare set slowly emerges in light, with a light blue backdrop. Wave noises in background (fading). Ludwig stands, looking out to the sea around him.

LUDWIG

These tides.

He reaches into his pockets, pulls out an old handkerchief.

Water has always calmed me...whilst also perplexing me. I comprehend its nature, its existence, but what of its value. It is soothing.

He dabs his eyes with his handkerchief.

I feel settled when I am on the water, especially in Norway... They were good days! I also feel a sense of comfort when I look out and see that turquoise blanket...somewhere to allow your body and thoughts to float. A damp, but pleasurable, bed for contemplation.

He walks a little to the left. He puts his head down. He is clearly upset.

I occasionally miss those who have played a part in shaping me; the person that is Ludwig Wittgenstein. Those that produced me: biologically. Those who shared my childhood; siblings who are similar but not the same...a leitmotif for humankind, I would argue.

He walks back and looks up.

Why are birds attracted to the seaside? Seagulls...everywhere. It is their territory. Their lives appear simple...though I can never ask them, and they would not be able to respond in any case. But they appear to be untroubled by life's trials and tribulations.

He contemplates.

Rhees could have accompanied me today...He is a sturdy prop. I would never term him an acolyte, but he listens to me and finds me bemusing and stimulating in equal measure. That is good for me. I find it hard to communicate with most people. They make me nervous, and I wish to block them. They look at me with some curiosity...quite often with unwarranted disdain. That is unpleasant, but they do not know me. They merely judge me at face value. That is a speculative verdict.

Silence.

I am happier solo...most of the time.

He looks out to sea.

Shall I publish again? Rhees wants me to...some at Cambridge also. I will...but not just yet.

He fiddles with his jacket, checks his pockets. He then looks up.

Those birds are constantly circling. Circling birds and ever-changing seas. A different form of continuity...but their actions represent a sense of permanency through generations and imitation. It is certainly not stability or stagnation!

He combs his hair back with his hand.

That lamb from yesterday was splendid. Rhees devoured it...I wonder what seagull tastes like?

He stares out again.

My mind is my camera.

He touches his head.

This creates my pictures. My pictures of my world.

He smiles and walks to one side. He stops then looks out again.

Ultimately, how can I make others aware of my view of the world? Are my facts their facts? They must be, but their understanding is not my understanding. There are too many imperfections.

He puts his hands together and pleads.

I need to know whether I see things that they do not. Do I experience matters that bypass them? Naturally, it is my choice if I walk into the water... I will get wet. If she is alongside me, then I know that Mrs Mann will get wet at the same time, but is her experience of the water at Langland Bay the same as mine? It would be different water, as we have established, but would she have the same feelings as I do from encountering the texture of the water? It would be at that moment, however, that she would come up against her greatest task. To put all her sensations into words that I could understand...

Looking and pointing up.

Not those seagulls...they cannot understand or speak...but I can!

He sighs heavily and puts his head to his chest.

My work is my life... The chain around my ankles.

He ponders.

Can it be solved? This riddle...this *raison d'être.*

He looks out to sea then buttons up his jacket.

Farewell sea!....Auf wiedersehen! That tide question, like all the rest, must wait.

Lights dim.

Music: *Haydn Serenade for strings Op. 3, No 5*

Act 2 Scene 5: *Swansea High Street Railway Station, 1940's (departure)*

Professor Rhyddid enters from the right and addresses the audience from the middle, which is lit in green and white.

PROFESSOR RHYDDID

There are times when every one of us must depart Swansea...to see loved ones, or for pastures new. For Wittgenstein leaving Swansea meant a return to Cambridge...back to the half-loved, half-hated day job...away from the beaches and back to the quads. He knew, or he assumed, that he would soon return to this "ugly, lovely town", that both inspires and at times infuriates. That refreshes, but sometimes restricts. That can be a breath of fresh air, if the wind is blowing in the right direction. So, what, ultimately, is it about this place...our place? This town that became a city. A city of song, surf...and a little bit of swearing. A city of poetry, prose, and philosophy. A city of invention and innovation...but not of innocence. A city of festivities and occasional frustrations. A city for you, a city for me...a city for Ludwig. But, for now, he departs.

Professor Rhyddid exits. The stage slowly lights up. Back at Swansea Railway Station. Ludwig has his suitcase in one hand. He is wearing the same jacket and trousers with which he arrived. He places his suitcase on the floor, and checks his jacket, He pulls out a ticket.

12.35 from Swansea to Cambridge via London…. I so wish it was the 12.34… that would be precise and sequential.

He continues to fumble in his pocket. He looks out.

Have I done what I came here to do?

Pauses.

If I have achieved anything, I can rest assured that Rhees will have jotted it down…. He is so supportive.

He looks again in his jacket.

I need to speak with a publisher…that is what Rhees told me. He is correct, again… I must write and disseminate…for everyone to appreciate.

He pulls the string out of his pocket, and stares at it for a few moments.

Objects are important to us at various times…do I need this to get on that train? Do I require it if an inspector asks to see my ticket? No and no, but it may be crucial if my shoelace snapped…So it has meaning, it has importance and it cannot be put to one side.

He puts it back in his pocket.

I must keep it. It will be needed.….perhaps very soon.

He looks again at his ticket.

Travel has played a key part in my life…. I do not like to stay too long in one place. It makes one creatively parched…. I will be back in Swansea soon…assuming that Rhees remains here. He is my point of contact… my kindred spirit and soul…A good companion, I feel.

He looks up to check the train times.

It is in. Arrived and ready to depart on time…. Is that an analogy for our lives? Will we depart this mortal coil on time? It may well be a time that is not of our reckoning. But would we wish to live forever…to extend our lives? Would we learn more? Learn more, think more, write more, lecture more. Can we do so in our limited time on this earth?

He looks at his ticket.

It is time! I have said farewell to Rhees, to Mrs Mann, to the Morgans, to the Clements and their delightful daughters, even to the sea… Did I remember the seagulls?… I will return. I like this place… it is not pretentious…. a town that reflects reality…with a quite beautiful hinterland. Rhees likes it too…that is vital for his happiness, his ideational process, and our friendship.

He looks up again at the timetable.

London it is…and then on to Cambridge. It will take several hours…I may get some sleep. I didn't manage too much in Cwmdonkin, nor did I during my time in Langland…too many thoughts…not enough time…

He pauses, raises his head, then lowers it.

There is never enough time! But I must confess... I am glad that I have been here.

He turns around, then smiles as the light goes down, and an image of the famous Wittgenstein photograph, taken in Swansea, appears in the background.

Music*: Ar Lan y Mor (harp)*

---*Diwedd*

www.ingramcontent.com/pod-product-compliance
Lightning Source LLC
Chambersburg PA
CBHW081258040426
42452CB00014B/2559